License to print money daily - OLuwaseyi Liadi

LICENSE TO PRINT MONEY DAILY.

(7 Things you must know if you must attract wealth)

Oluwaseyi Liadi

Copyright © August 2022 by Oluwaseyi Liadi

All rights reserved. No part of this book may be reproduced, distributed, or transmitted in any form or by any means, including photocopying, recording, or other electronic, digital, or mechanical methods, without the prior written permission of the publisher, except in the case of brief quotations embodied in critical reviews and certain other non-commercial uses permitted by copyright law.

Published by Beacon Publishers
Beakonglobal@gmail.com
+2348103271948

DEDICATION

To the Creator of Heaven and Earth, the giver of Light and Wisdom.

Table of Contents

Title Page
Copyright Page
Dedication

PREAMBLE 2
INTRODUCTION 2
CHAPTER ONE 2
WHAT ARE YOU SELLING? 2
CHAPTER TWO 2
DO YOU HAVE A BUSINESS MINDSET? 2
CHAPTER THREE 2
YOU CAN MAGNETIZE WEALTH 2
CHAPTER FOUR 2
YOU NEED THE WEALTH GENERATORS 2
FINAL WORD 2
YOUR THOUGHT IS A MAGNET 2
Table of Contents 1

PREAMBLE

The beauty of this 21st century is that everything is possible. Yes, you can read that again. We have left the era where impossibility used to be a regular cliché. This is an information era.
Information is now the new currency.

Living your dream life is not as difficult as before, you just have to plug in and lay your hands on the needed information and boom, you will be living in your dreamland. You can break barriers.

We live in a borderless world, where information now flows around the world without barriers.

You must understand that wealth is not an exclusive right of the selected caucus.

Permit me to say that, the poor of this century are not a person who can not read nor write, but the ones who have willingly decided to ignore knowledge.

I was not born with a silver spoon in my mouth. I can't even remember if I was born with any spoon in my mouth. One thing I am sure of is that I tasted poverty in the past and today I enjoy wealth. The difference is clear.

This book will show you how you can make your wealthy dream a reality.

My state of wealth today was determined by the discovery I

made. I am glad to let you know that access to clean wealth has been democratized.

This book is aimed at doing a few things.
1. To give you a proven blueprint, to attract and retain wealth.
2. To reveal how you can be positioned, not to pursue money, but to attract wealth.

3. Educating you on how to create more streams of income.

4. Placing in your hands some major tools of wealth creation. Fasten your seatbelt, as we go on this wealthy journey.

After you finish this book, you will have no excuse to remain poor.

INTRODUCTION

If you are poor, your family will turn against you, and your friends will avoid you

even more. You might beg them for help, but no one will come to help you. - Holy Bible
Poverty is a repellant, while wealth is magnetic. Wealth is a state of abundance of all good things in life. Wealth is good and its effect is desirable by many.

To be wealthy is beyond having plenty of money. Wealthiness is likened to a tree with branches, such as healthy living, being valuable, enjoying peace and fulfillment, having good relationships, full of ideas and money.

To be healthy is to be wealthy. Good health is an asset. A dead man can not do business.

Wealth is a mindset! Your mind is a place for processing thoughts and feelings. Whatever you permit to be processed in your mind, will become your reality on the ground.

Who you are today, is the product of your exposure to

information, training, and knowledge deposited by the environment. This eventually formed your mindset.

Your mindset, therefore, is a habitual or characteristic mental attitude, that defines how you will interpret and respond to situations in life.

Wealth begins from your mind, not from your pocket. I became wealthy on the inside before I attracted wealth on the outside. My first car was magnetized by my thoughts, and I used the same car for about four years.
What are you thinking about right now?
Wrong mindsets are viruses. They corrupt a good mind and limit progress. For you to attract wealth, you must deliberately become a murderer of toxic thoughts.

For instance, in Africa, people say things like: **Money does not grow on trees**. This is not correct.

Many grew up with the mentality, that the reason poverty is an everyday experience, is that 'money does not grow on a tree. I am sure you have heard that before. But I am here to defy that.

The new knowledge is that MONEY NOW GROWS ON TREES, depending on the kind of seed you plant! I plant my 'money seed' on a daily basis! Whatever information you plant, in your thoughts today, you will reap in your life tomorrow. You can continuously print your own money, simply by planting the money seed.

You need money to make money.
You also hear people say that you need money to make money. This is not absolutely true. When you operate with this wrong mindset, you will be limited in creativity. You don't need money to birth great ideas. Any barrier

created in your thought realm is self-made.

Experience has taught me that, when I have an idea to execute, I don't start with the capital (money) needed to fuel it. I will do all I need to do in terms of planning, making research, talking to the right people about the possibility of the idea, preparing myself for the actualization of such an idea, and then I will talk about how to source the money last. I have discovered that when an idea 'consumes' you, it will eventually attract capital. Vision attracts provision.

Money is the root of evil.

Let me address this with the thought of Reno Omokri. *'Money is never evil. Money spreads the Gospel. Money builds hospitals. Money feeds the hungry. Money pays for medical research. Do you know what is evil? Poverty. Because it steals your health, kills your peace, and destroys your dreams. Make money so you can do good!' (Reno Omokri)*

CHAPTER ONE

WHAT ARE YOU SELLING?

Any attempt to attract wealth or money into your life without the readiness to part with a valuable item or service is an act of injustice. Making money from people without offering a product or worthy service is simply extortion. Any effort you make in attracting wealth, without a willingness to serve people, might end up in futility. It is simply a waste of time.

Praying for money, without the willingness to render a valuable service or product is an act of innocent begging or harmless thievery (robbery).

My question is what are you selling? Product or Service?

What is a BUSINESS?

A Business is an act of exchanging your service or your product for the money.
It is a process of exchange of value. The money received from a business enterprise is not a gift. It's a reward.

A reward is a payment made in return for a service, goodwill or product rendered for satisfaction.

Is Your 'Busyness' A Business?

Many claim to be busy, yet they are broke. Channeling your effort into creating values for others will make you a money magnet. People pay for value. They don't pay for gossip. You must constantly review your daily activities. Track your minutes. Track your hours. Track your day.

What do you spend most of your day doing? In life, there are three ways for you to use your time. Some spend their time.

Some waste their time and others invest their time.

Whatever you do with your time today, will determine what your life will give to you tomorrow. So, you must track how you spend your day. If the activities you engage in on a daily basis are not adding up to your wealth, then change them.

Problem Produces Wealth

To attract wealth, you must master the process of converting problems into money.

Bayo Omoboriowo's journey from grass to grace is the best fit to illustrate the above caption. A young man that was raised in the Mushin area of Lagos state (Nigeria) and in just a matter of few years, rose to become the official photographer of the Nigerian President, since 2015, till date.

Narrating his story in an interview with Citipeople Magazine, he said, *" I am an ardent newspaper reader and I look at it, and mostly, many photographs in the papers are political photographs. The photographs portraying the President or Governors, I saw as bad photographically. I saw that there was a gap and someone needed to fill that gap.*

Brilliant photographers were not involved in political photography. So, I found a need and I was ready to solve the problem. So, that was what took me from being a documentary photographer, to a photojournalist and that was why I went to Ekiti, Osun and Lagos State, without being paid to be following political figures up and down."

This young man, who is in his thirties, found a problem that is linked to his passion. He went after the problem, with a solution. When he was presented to Gen. Buhari (Nigerian President), he stood out among all others, simply because there was a need that needed to be filled up. What need can you fill up in this world?

Listen to me, when you provide a solution to a millionaire's problem, you will gain access to his millions. Don't focus on what you will get from a millionaire, locate a vacuum you need to fill up for him.

Bayo Omoboriowo has been flying about in the Nigerian presidential convoy for more than seven years, simply because he is consistently solving a problem for the president. The problem you can solve will naturally create a space for you at the top.

What problem(s) can you solve?

1. _____
_____
___

2. _____
_____
___

3. _____
_____
___

4. _____
_____
___

Action Points

1. List on paper what you can sell to earn money.
2. Find out the service you can exchange for money. Either what you know before or a new one.
3. Don't just spend your day, invest your time. Do something profitable daily.
4. Locate a problem around you and get a skill to supply the solution.

CHAPTER TWO

DO YOU HAVE A BUSINESS MINDSET?

Life, by nature, was designed for interaction, not for isolation. Interaction is the transfer of words, ideas, gestures, thoughts, products, and other elements (material or immaterial) to others. Looking at this, you can conclude that life is built for business.

Business involves exchange! Life is a business. From time immemorial, the business has been a vital initiative. I learned that the first one-cent coin in the United States was minted in 1787, named the Fugio cent. Fugio cent was designed by Benjamin Franklin. On the coin, was the picture of the sun and a caption with the words 'MIND YOUR BUSINESS' meaning 'time flies, do your work.

Even now, in the 21st century, the caption is still relevant. Time flies. Do your business!
Business mentality, therefore, is the mindset that is concerned about exchanging products or services with others in need of such for monetary gain.

I am sure you have been paid in the past for rendering one productive activity or the other. If you have given a product to someone in the past and you received the money in return, then you have engaged in business.

Business people are value creators.

Business people are solution providers.

Business people are problem-solvers.

If you must attract wealth, you must think business! An employee focuses on his or her salary, while an employer (businessman) focuses on problems to be converted to a continuous wealth funnel.

Let me give you a few reasons why you should consider going into business.

1. **Best way to BUILD WEALTH**

   Business people are wealth creators. A business fellow can initiate a new product to tackle a certain problem which in turn will add money to his bank account. Money comes to you in proportion to the problems you can solve. If you can become a business owner, you will hardly run out of money. The more creative you are, in creating a solution to people's needs, the fatter your bank account will be.

2. **Your TIME is under your control.** Time is life. He that is in control of your time, is literally in control of your life. A businessman has control over his time. You can choose to meet your client in the morning or later in the day. An employee can hardly control his time. The organization is in control of his time because the salary being paid is not only for his service but also for his time. Listen to me, no one can place value on your time as accurately as you would do, if you are into business.

3. **You provide EMPLOYMENT Opportunities.**

Unemployment rate increases in many countries, especially third world countries, because we have more job seekers than job makers. When you go into a business, you will become a job creator. The degree of your wealth is not in cash you stash in banks all over the world, but by the impact you can make in the lives of others.

As a business person, when you employ one person, you are invariably responsible for the well-being of his wife and children through the payment of his salary. For instance, the day I fail to pay the salary of my workers, their children might go to bed hungry and they can be denied access to school because of non-payment of tuition. The world will stand still if they are no business people.

4. **You Create PRODUCTS or SERVICES that add VALUE to people's lives.**

A business owner creates valuable products and services for the benefit of mankind. When you are a business owner, your productivity satisfies people's desires. Your existence in the business world gives fulfillment to many. Just imagine for a moment, if no one produces the phone, tablet, or laptop you are using right now, what medium will you use to meet exactly the needs the gadgets are meeting presently? That is the reason, you should go into business. The more businesses we have, the more satisfaction we will enjoy in this world.

5. **You will add to your COUNTRY'S WEALTH.**
Being a business owner will afford you the privilege to become a contributor to your country's wealth. This is reflected in the National income or GDP (Gross domestic product). This is the reason; an intelligent government supports the establishment of businesses. A successful business will surely pay

more tax, which in turn, adds to government revenue.

6. **As a business owner, you cannot be FIRED!**
Covid 19 challenged the sustainability of many businesses, and as a result of the mandatory lockdown, many businesses were grounded. Downsizing was a natural thing for many business organizations to stay alive. Most employees were fired! But many business owners were not fired but hibernated. Now, in the Post-Covid era, those business owners have resurfaced with new-normal strategies.

It's more secure to be a businessman than to be an employee.

Action Points

1. Don't just exchange words with your network, begin to exchange products or services.
2. Think about a specific business to start this week. You can start small as I did

grow big afterward. Talk to me about this.
3. Start your business this month.
4. Be determined to become a job creator. Your decision to be a job maker will drive you into the business world.

CHAPTER THREE

YOU CAN MAGNETIZE WEALTH

Cambridge dictionary defines a magnet as an object, that can attract iron and steel obje cts.

A person is said to be magnetic if things, objects, and people feel strongly attrac ted to him.

A magnet can either attract or repel an object. The size of the magnet will determine what the magnet can attract. The power inherent in the magnet will determine the degree of attraction.

Wealth can be attracted.
You can magnetize wealth. Wealth and riches can be attracted to you, once you are empowered to be a magnet. How can you be empowered to attract wealth?

• Discover YOURSELF: Find your PASSION

You've got to find yourself first. Everything else follow - Charles de Lint
Knowing yourself is the beginning of your life.

Inside you lie the answer to the questions being asked by your world. Locate 'you' within yourself.

Listening to a Nigerian-born real estate mogul, Ayilara Olawale (CEO, Landwey Properties), He recounted how he moved from being a failure in several businesses to a celebrated business magnate. He stated that one

of the keys that helped him was 'Know yourself
Knowing yourself is a process of unveiling your strength and your passion. It is the process of finding your voice. It is about locating your place of gift (service).

Connecting your passion with people's problems in a bid to provide solutions, will command wealth into your life. Discover money-making activities around your passion and explore them for your profit.

Bayo Omoboriowo uncovered his passion and converted it into a wealth magnet. Before he became Nigeria's president photographer, he had been working tirelessly in line with his passion which is photography. He is unarguably one of the youthful office holders in Aso rock, if not the youngest. He became President Buhari's personal photographer at the age of 28 years after being his photographer for all his campaign rallies. (citipeopleonline.com).

Your discovered Passion will supply your energy. You can deploy your energy in meeting people's needs to fuel your pocket.

Use SWOT to discover yourself.

S - Strength
W - Weakness
O - Opportunities
T - Threats

Pick a clean piece of paper and write out what you do well and what you love to do. Inside your strength lies your wealth. Your discovered strength, if well maximized, will magnetize your money. Write out your weaknesses as well and seek to quench them. What are the threats to your strengths? Answer this question and tackle them.

Finally, look around you to realize the opportunities that need the expression of your strength. By your strength, you can be made wealthy. You need to get this: <u>From passion to profit</u>

- **Locate a PROBLEM to solve.**
Problems are money in disguise. The ability to solve a problem is a necessity to attract wealth into your life. Stop seeing problems as problems.
In the business world, problems are convertible currency. The problem is a route to making money. One of the best ways to make money is by converting people's problems into your source of wealth. The problem produces pain. People pay to remove pain. Let me give you an example, the greatest problem in life is a spiritual problem. Next to a spiritual problem, is a family problem. After a family problem, it is a health problem and the list goes on. If you can sit down and design a solution to people's pressing problems, you won't need to force them before they part with their money.

People pay when they are in need. If you can discover what people need around you and design a solution that will fill the need. Then you will get the money from them without coercion. That's why business people love problems. I love problems. If you want to attract wealth you must love problems. Once you are operating from a business perspective, you will specialize in designing solutions. *'Since problems no dey finish, business sef no go finish'*

For instance, in our companies, we focused on solving clothing problems, shelter problems and ignorance problems. We have been doing these for many years and we are growing stronger by the day.

Have you observed that people call or message you when there is a need you need to help them resolve? If you are not solving problems, you are not needed!

- **Acquire KNOWLEDGE**

The world we live in is framed by the word. Information is the wheel of life. Information is the lifeblood of the entire world. If you check your routine on a daily basis, you will discover that you run with knowledge. Life without information will be lopsided.

What you know can put money into your account. Acquiring knowledge is not only for consumption value. It is also for creating value, which will consistently boost your earning capacity.

Tuition Fees Are Not Negotiable.

The ability to sell knowledge is a good way to build wealth. We are in the knowledge economy. This implies that what you know (if well packaged and presented to the right people) will put money in your pocket. I observed that right from my primary school days till my university days, school fees are not usually negotiable. The school determines the price. The system is the same, when you go to a doctor for consultation, he consults you, based on his acquired knowledge. Consultation is not for free as well.

• **Become An Information Merchant**

People who sell information to others for their capacity enlargement are value creators. You can become an 'information merchant'. Be a content creator. They use their knowledge-capacity to attract wealth. You can sell information. There's information about something you know, that someone else does not know. Learn how to package what you know for others who need them to buy. Your knowledge is your tool of wealth. I discovered that even your past mistakes can attract wealth into your life. Write down your past mistakes in the form of fiction. Extract the morals in the mistakes and suggest better ways to avoid such errors. Put them in a book and you will be amazed how people will respond positively to purchase. I am sure nobody wants to live a life of regular errors. There is something you can sell, check within you.

• **Learn a SKILL**

After my first degree, I deliberately went to acquire tailoring skills. This singular skill made me lots of money.

Skill refers to the ability to do something well. Skill is the knowledge and ability that enables one to do something well as a result of training or practice.

Skill can be referred to a type of work or craft that requires special training and experience to do well.

A few days ago, I watched a video on youtube, where a Nigerian lady, a resident in the United Kingdom, was educating the minds of people who desire to relocate to the United Kingdom. She advised that if you chose to live and work in the United Kingdom, you had better acquire certain skills from your home country. She mentioned skills such as, Cooking and Catering, Driving, Plumbing, Carpentry, Photography,

Hairdressing, Barbing, Sewing, Furniture, Bricklaying, Electricals, Interior Decoration etc. Some people until now held a mindset that the aforementioned skills are domestically useful but internationally useless. *This is an incorrect statement.*

The influence of technology in this 21st century is massive. As a result of this, there are what we now call high-paying skills or high-income skills. A high-income skill is a skill that will make you a large income. In other words, high-paying skills are those abilities that can make you a seven-figure income, even if you don't have a university degree. These skills are predominantly digital. *Some examples of such platforms and skills are as follows Cryptocurrency trader, YouTube, Fiverr, Quora, Amazon Kindle Publishing, Social Media Management, Instagram ads, Project Writing, Upwork, Coding, Digital Marketer, Shopify,*

Affiliate Marketing, Survey Junkie, CashKarma, Problogging, Proofreadanywhere, Virtual PA, OnlineTutor, Podcaster, Music, ReviewApps, CreatorSEO, Consulting, Facebook ads, Google ads, Instagram ads consultant, Graphics design, Video animation, copywriting, Web development, Web design, Digital marketing, Cloud computing, Mobile apps development, and Video editing, Coding and so on.

Action Points

1. Don't just exchange words with your network (people), begin to exchange products or services.
2. Think about a specific business to start this week. You can start small as I did, you will grow big afterward. Talk to me on this. Start your business this month.
3. Go and learn a skill today. Add to your skills in order to earn more.
4. Be determined to become a job creator. *(Your decision*

to be a job maker will drive you into the business world).

CHAPTER FOUR

YOU NEED THE WEALTH GENERATORS

Wealth generators are the catalysts for generating wealth. Out of many, I will share only a few. These are God, Google, and YouTube.

GOD

'People might plan what they want to say, but it is the Lord who gives them the right words.

In life, there are things under your control. There are things you can not control. Trying to control what you are not meant to control is a cheap definition of frustration.

For instance, you can't control

the weather! You can only align your preparation with the weather.

You truly need God to influence what is beyond you. For by strength shall no man prevail.
I have seen something else under the sun: King Solomon remarked in the bible that the race is not to the swift or the battle to the strong, nor does food come to the wise or wealth to the brilliant or favour to the learned; but time and chance happen to them all.

God is sovereign. In all your getting, prioritize your relationship with God. Irrespective of your diverse efforts, He will eventually determine the result and the reward. You must note that business is warfare, not a fun fare, get God involved from the beginning.

GOOGLE
According to Techopedia 'Google is an internet search

engine. It uses a proprietary algorithm that's designed to retrieve and order search results to provide the most relevant and dependable sources of data possible. It

Google's stated mission is to "organize the world's information and make it universally accessible and useful." It is the top search engine in the world, a position that has generated criticism and concern about the power it has to influence the flow of online information.

Google is a one-stop internet hub for a myriad of information. The beginning of any successful money-making activity is access to the right information. I use google countless times on a daily basis. As I write my books, I check words on google regularly. It gives my writing the global cutting edge. Through Google, you can access the fresh thoughts and submissions of various people on the planet, right from your location.

There is information you don't need to ask God. Just google it! There are a lot of opportunities for amassing durable wealth in the world. Learning to use google will open you up to several ways to attract wealth.

YOUTUBE
YouTube is a video-sharing social media where users watch, like, share, comment, and upload their videos. Youtube platform is the best video social media.

YouTube is an American online video-sharing platform headquartered in San Bruno, California, founded by three former PayPal employees- Chad Hurley, Steve Chen, and Jawed Karim– in February 2005.
Google bought the site in November 2006 for US$1.65 billion, since which it operates as one of

Google's subsidiaries. (Wikipedia)
Youtube is the contemporary virtual university of this century. There is hardly anything you can't learn via videos on youtube. Go and master how to use YouTube profitably. You will rake in cash, while you are asleep.

How can you make money from YouTube? You can make money from YouTube, through a YouTube partner program, brand sponsorship, fan funding, advertising, affiliate marketing, sales, and so on.

According to statistics, In 2021, it was calculated that YouTube Mr. Beast (Jimmy Donaldson) ranked first as the top-earning YouTuber worldwide with annual earnings of approximately 54 million U.S. dollars (about 22 billion naira). Jake Paul ranked second, with an estimate of 45 million U.S. dollars (about 19 billion naira).

In Nigeria, the highest-paid Youtuber is Mark Angel, the founder of Mark Angel Comedy. He was born in 1991 in Port Harcourt, Nigeria. He became the first African comedian to amass one million subscribers in 2017. He is estimated to be worth 3.8 million U.S. dollars (about 1.7 billion naira). His monthly earnings is approximately 326,800 U.S. dollars (about 138 million naira).

Other top earners in Nigeria include:
- Editorial Natural beauty 556 (Beauty)
- Broda Shaggi (Comedy)
- Toke Makinwa (Relationship)
- Kassim Bramah (Comedy)
- Taooma Cabin (Comedy)
- Eric Okafor (Tech reviews)

Your name can be added to the above names. Get out of your limiting zone. Dig deep into your inner self. Dig out the right solution to people's problems, package it, offer it for sale and money will be looking for you.

| Action Points |

1. Don't just hustle to make money, involve God! Face God, before you face any business.
2. Take advantage of the internet through the use of Google.
3. If you must earn more and scale your business, start leveraging the use of Youtube.
4. Select your niche (area) and learn how to create content on Youtube. Become a YouTuber!

FINAL WORD

YOUR THOUGHT IS A MAGNET

'If you stay in a quiet place and think undisturbed for 15 minutes about money, you will get money-making ideas. Wealthy people do it. It is

called ideating. But people with a poverty mentality will NEVER do this. Instead, they will criticize what they have not tried!' - Reno Omokri

As a man thinks, so is he. Your wealth must first be created in your heart before it appears in your hand.

The root of every reformation lies in the realm of imagination.

'Just as the OAK TREE develops from the herm (seed) that lies in the ACORN, and the BIRDS develops from the germ that lies asleep in the EGG, so will your MATERIAL ACHIEVEMENTS grow out of the organized plans that you create in your IMAGINATION..'-Napoleon hill

Great works are products of deep thoughts!

Thinking is hard work! Using your imagination requires diligence. Think your way through. Your Imagination is an asset in the world of creativity.

Everything good invention you see today was once a thought in someone's imagination.

What is your present thought that will add value to the human race?
Whatever your mind can conceive, whatever your mind can believe, with the right effort, your hand will surely receive. A mental handicap is more terrible than a physical handicap. Every journey in life begins with an internal trip.
You can attract the wealth you desire if you can filter your heart. Get rid of wealth-limiting mindsets. Furnish your heart with healthy and wealthy thoughts, you will soon be living the wealthy life you once envisioned!

See you at the top!
Make big plans, don't make small plans, big plans attract big people, small plans attract

small people, and small people cause big problems.

-Former French Prime Minister-

OTHER DIGITAL BOOKS BY THE AUTHOR

- How to be Smarter than Scammers

  https://selar.co/Smarterthanscammers
  (amazon) https://amzn.to/3dHtYIP

- 13 Potent Laws of Academic Excellence
  Get Yours

CONNECT WITH THE AUTHOR
Facebook : Instagram : Twitter
(Oluwaseyiliadi)
Email : oluwaseyiliadi@gmail.com
Whatsapp : +2348053052772

About The Author

Oluwaseyi Liadi is loaded with a passion to impact lives at all levels. He is a positive influencer and a passionate leader with an intense desire to raise an informed generation where human potential is optimally maximized and a high premium is placed on knowledge for a strong and influential society.

He is certified as a leadership trainer under the tutelage of Sam Adeyemi at the Daystar leadership academy where he obtained basic and advanced leadership training.

He is the founder of infomeal consulting, an organization founded to nourish human minds with needful information. Through this medium, he organized seminars for youths and young adults.

He is a staunch entrepreneur. He founded Sterlingbrains Biz Dealings with divisions in Fashion, Real Estate and Project Development.

Oluwaseyi (fondly called Seyiwealth) is a life coach, conference speaker, creative thinker, Leadership Consultant, serial entrepreneur, and a writer who is happily married to a beautiful princess; Abimbola Liadi (an educator), and they are blessed with excellent children, Daniel and Daniella.

www.ingramcontent.com/pod-product-compliance
Lightning Source LLC
Chambersburg PA
CBHW050319220526
45465CB00005B/2055